Mohlolo:

An original Novel by **Lebohang Phoshudi & Lebohang Xavier Poetry**

Mohlolo: In the Shadows of Hope

Mohlolo, Volume 1

Lebohang Xavier Poetry and Lebohang Phoshuli

Published by P&M Publishers, 2023.

MOHLOLO: IN THE SHADOWS OF HOPE

First edition. July 25, 2023.

ISBN: 979-8223990512

Written by Lebohang Xavier Poetry and Lebohang Phoshuli.

Table of Contents

Mohlolo: In the Shadows of Hope 1

Chapter 1 3

Chapter 2 8

Chapter 3 12

Chapter 4 16

Chapter 5 18

Chapter 6 20

Chapter 7 23

Chapter 8 27

Chapter 9 30

Chapter 10 33

Chapter 12 37

Chapter 13 39

Chapter 14 41

Chapter 15 45

Chapter 16 54

Chapter 17 58

Preface:

In the pages that follow, I invite you to embark on a journey—a journey of resilience, love, and self-discovery. This book is a testament to the power of the human spirit, to the capacity for growth and transformation even in the face of adversity.

Within these chapters, you will find the story of a young soul navigating the twists and turns of life, weaving through moments of heartache, loss, and despair. But amidst the darkness, there is also light—the light of love, friendship, and the unwavering support of those who believe in the protagonist's potential.

This book is a tapestry of experiences, a mosaic of emotions, and a celebration of the human connections that shape our lives. It is a reflection on the power of love, both in its capacity to heal wounds and ignite dreams. It is a testament to the resilience of the human spirit, as it rises from the depths of despair to embrace the beauty of life's journey.

Through the eyes of our protagonist, we witness the bonds of family, the unwavering loyalty of friends, and the impact of mentors who guide and inspire. We delve into the depths of grief and emerge with newfound strength and purpose. We experience the joy of first love and the challenges of navigating relationships. And ultimately, we witness the transformative power of love—love that mends broken hearts, love that nurtures dreams, and love that carries us through the darkest of times.

As you turn the pages, I encourage you to immerse yourself in the story, to walk alongside the characters as they navigate the complexities of life. May you find solace in their triumphs, inspiration in their resilience, and wisdom in their reflections.

This is a story of hope—a reminder that even in our most vulnerable moments, we possess the strength to rise, to rebuild, and to create a future filled with love and purpose. It is my hope that this tale will touch your heart, ignite your own resilience, and remind you of the transformative power of love.

So, let us begin this journey together, where the power of love, the resilience of the human spirit, and the beauty of self-discovery intertwine to create a narrative that will stay with you long after you turn the final page.

Chapter 1

In the cozy confines of our small four-roomed house, my family and I found solace amidst the limitations of space. Living with my parents, my older sister Noni, my younger sister Thatelo, and myself, we made the most of what we had. Our home may not have been extravagant, but it was a place where love and resilience thrived.

As the only boy, I claimed the sofa as my sleeping spot, while my sisters shared a bedroom, their laughter and sisterly bond echoing through the walls. During festive seasons, when our extended family came to visit, we would gladly rearrange the furniture, creating makeshift beds on the floor to accommodate everyone. Those nights were filled with joy and laughter, creating memories that still bring a smile to my face.

Winter posed its challenges, but my resourceful parents always found a way to keep us warm. I can still recall the scent of illuminating paraffin that my father brought home to fuel the heater, a humble device that emanated a comforting warmth throughout our home. It was a testament to my parents' ingenuity and determination to provide for us, even in the face of limited resources.

Our family, although not affluent, was content and held in high regard within our community. We presented a united front, radiating decency and grace. From the outside, we appeared to be the epitome of a perfect family, but life has a way of revealing the hidden struggles behind closed doors.

One fateful morning, our lives took an unexpected turn. Noni, my beloved older sister, fell ill, complaining of a persistent stomach ache and a fever that refused to break. As a family rooted in tradition, my mother turned to the remedies of our culture, preparing a dilute Aloe concoction to ease Noni's discomfort. However, my father, ever the pragmatic thinker, harbored concerns. Deep down, he felt it was time to seek professional medical assistance.

This decision marked a departure from our usual routines. Together, my parents made the choice to delve into their hard-earned savings to finance a trip to a private medical practice. Dr. O. Mohammed, a respected surgeon in town, held the key to unlocking the mystery behind Noni's ailment. I yearned to accompany them, curious to witness the world of medicine unfold before my eyes. But my parents, conscious of the financial burden and wanting to ensure Thatelo's care, insisted that I stay behind.

Left in the solitude of our home, the weight of responsibility fell upon me. With my parents' departure, I assumed the role of caretaker, looking after Thatelo's well-being. As we stood at the door, anticipation filled the air, and a mischievous idea took hold of my imagination. In hushed whispers, I shared my plan with Thatelo. We would embark on our own adventure, following in our parents' footsteps once they had left, discovering the world outside our haven.

Thatelo's eyes sparkled with excitement, and she eagerly agreed to our secret escapade. We understood the need for discretion, ensuring our journey remained hidden from our parents' watchful eyes. When Thatelo inquired about our destination, I couldn't resist playfully teasing her about seeing her friend Karabo. Her enthusiastic response assured me that our shared adventure was sealed.

Unbeknownst to us, this impromptu journey would become a turning point in our lives. Little did we realize the secrets, revelations, and extraordinary experiences that awaited us beyond the confines of our familiar four-roomed house.

As I stood at the door, ready to embark on our clandestine adventure, a flood of memories washed over me, taking me back to the day Thatelo first entered our lives. It was a day of joy and transformation, a day that forever altered the dynamics of our family.

I vividly remember the excitement that permeated the air as my parents returned home with a precious bundle in their arms. Thatelo, a tiny and delicate newborn, had captured our hearts from the moment we laid eyes on her. The house, once filled with three voices, now echoed with the innocent cooing of a baby.

My parents, with their eyes brimming with love and tenderness, embraced Thatelo as if she had always been a part of us. They showered her with affection, providing her with a warm and nurturing environment. Noni, being the doting sister that she was, took on the role of Thatelo's protector, always by her side and ensuring her comfort.

For me, as the older brother, it was a remarkable moment of responsibility and pride. I promised myself that I would be the best brother Thatelo could ever have. I would watch over her, guide her, and ensure that she would never feel alone in this world.

The days turned into weeks, and weeks into months, as we all settled into our newfound roles within the family. Thatelo grew, her infectious laughter filling our home with joy. She became the beacon of light that brought us closer together, forging an unbreakable bond.

As I looked at Thatelo now, her eyes gleaming with anticipation, I couldn't help but feel a surge of protectiveness. I wanted to shield her from the harsh realities of the world, to preserve her innocence for as long as possible. But I also knew that life had a way of teaching us invaluable lessons, molding us into the resilient individuals we were meant to become.

With a shared understanding and a secret pact between us, Thatelo and I set out on our adventure, fueled by curiosity and the desire to experience life beyond our small haven. Little did we know that this journey would test our resilience, push us to our limits, and ultimately shape us into the people we were destined to be.

As we ventured into the unknown, I couldn't help but feel a mix of apprehension and excitement. We were stepping out of the familiar, embracing the uncertainty of the world outside our four-roomed house.

What lay ahead would challenge us, strengthen us, and ultimately define us.

Little did we know that our lives were about to change in ways we could never have imagined. The adventures, the trials, and the triumphs that awaited us would mold us into individuals with stories to tell, lessons to learn, and a resilience that would carry us through the darkest of times.

As we took that first step beyond the threshold of our home, I couldn't help but feel a sense of gratitude for the foundation that my parents had laid. Their love, guidance, and unwavering support would forever be etched in our hearts as we navigated the unpredictable journey ahead.

ooooooooooooooooooooo

With newfound determination and a shared sense of purpose, Thatelo and I tackled our chores with remarkable speed and efficiency. It was as if our unspoken mission had ignited a spark within us, propelling us forward with unwavering focus.

As I swept the floors, Thatelo diligently washed the dishes, and together we tidied our small haven, leaving no corner untouched. We worked in harmony, synchronized in our actions, and for the first time, it felt like we were truly seeing eye to eye. The bond between us grew stronger with each passing moment, bridging the gap between siblings and creating a sense of unity that we had longed for.

Completing our tasks ahead of schedule, we stood at the door, giddy with anticipation. The world lay before us, ready to be explored and experienced. Adventure beckoned, and we were eager to embrace it with open arms.

With a mischievous grin, I whispered to Thatelo, "Are you ready for the grand escapade?" Her eyes sparkled with excitement as she nodded enthusiastically. We locked the door behind us, leaving our small haven for a brief moment, venturing into the vastness of the world beyond.

Little did we know that this adventure would be just the beginning of a series of extraordinary journeys. Together, Thatelo and I would navigate the twists and turns, the highs and lows, all while strengthening the unbreakable bond we shared as siblings.

As we stepped into the unknown, hand in hand, we awaited the adventures that awaited us. The world was our playground, and we were ready to explore every nook and cranny, to learn, to grow, and to create memories that would last a lifetime.

With hearts filled with excitement and minds brimming with curiosity, we set forth, united in our quest for discovery. The future was uncertain, but with each step we took, we knew that we were capable of overcoming any challenge that lay in our path.

And so, we embarked on this grand escapade, ready to face the world, hand in hand, siblings bound by love and a shared hunger for life's greatest adventures.

Chapter 2

The sun shone brightly as I walked down the familiar path that led to the home of my best friend, Pontsho. Our houses were separated by a mere fence, and growing up, we had developed a bond that went beyond mere friendship. It was a connection that made our childhood adventures all the more exciting.

As I reached the gate, I could hear the laughter and playful chatter of children. Pontsho had a younger sister named Prudence, who was the same age as my sister, Thatelo. The two of them were inseparable, just like Pontsho and I.

Entering their yard, I spotted Pontsho and Prudence playing behind a small shack backroom. Their laughter echoed through the air, filling me with a sense of joy. I couldn't help but smile at the sight of their carefree spirits.

"Pontsho! Prudence!" I called out, drawing their attention. They turned towards me, their faces lighting up with excitement. We exchanged quick glances that conveyed the unspoken understanding of a new adventure about to unfold.

Pontsho was a tall and lanky boy, with a mischievous glint in his eyes. He had a knack for finding hidden treasures and secrets within the confines of our small neighborhood. Prudence, on the other hand, was a bright and spirited girl, full of curiosity and a thirst for exploration, just like my sister Thatelo.

"Guess what, Mohlolo?" Pontsho exclaimed, his voice brimming with excitement. "Prudence and I have discovered something incredible behind this little backroom!"

My curiosity piqued, I asked eagerly, "What is it? Tell me everything!"

Pontsho motioned for us to gather closer, leaning in as he shared the details of their recent discovery. Behind the backroom, there was a small, hidden garden. It was a modest patch of green amidst the urban landscape, filled with flourishing plants and colorful blooms. The garden was a serene oasis, tucked away from the hustle and bustle of everyday life.

"The garden is magical, Mohlolo," Prudence chimed in, her eyes shining with wonder. "We've been growing vegetables and flowers here. It's like having our secret paradise right in our own backyard!"

My heart raced with anticipation. A hidden garden right next door? It sounded like a hidden gem waiting to be explored. The thought of embarking on this new adventure with Pontsho and Prudence filled me with excitement and a sense of wonder.

"Can we go there now?" I asked, unable to contain my eagerness.

Pontsho nodded, his grin widening. "Of course! Let's grab some tools and see what new surprises await us in our secret garden."

As we gathered gardening tools and gloves, I couldn't help but feel a surge of gratitude for the close-knit community we were a part of. Our neighbors, Pontsho and Prudence, were not just friends but extended family to us.

With the anticipation of new discoveries dancing in our hearts, we stepped into the hidden garden, ready to explore its wonders. Little did we know that this simple backyard oasis would become a place of countless adventures, nurturing our spirits and forging memories that would last a lifetime.

As Pontsho and I got our hands dirty, tending to the plants and sowing new seeds, our conversation naturally drifted towards deeper topics. We discussed our dreams, our aspirations, and the challenges we faced in a world that often seemed filled with obstacles.

Pontsho shared his passion for science and his desire to make a difference through research and innovation. I talked about my love for literature and how I dreamed of becoming a teacher, inspiring young minds and empowering them with knowledge.

Our conversations in the garden were not like the idle chatter of ordinary children. We discussed the power of education, the importance of community, and the resilience needed to overcome obstacles. Together, we discovered new perspectives, nurturing a sense of curiosity and empathy within ourselves.

As we toiled away, we found solace in the quiet beauty of the garden. The gentle breeze carried the sweet scent of blooming flowers, and the sunlight filtered through the leaves, casting a dappled glow on our faces. In that little corner of the world, we were free to be ourselves, to dream, and to grow.

As the hours slipped by, we marveled at the progress we had made. The once barren soil now teemed with life, with vibrant greens and bursts of color. We had transformed the neglected corner of our backyard into a sanctuary of growth and beauty.

With dirt-stained hands and smiles on our faces, we knew that the hidden garden had become a sacred space for us. It was more than just a patch of land; it was a reflection of our friendship, our dreams, and our shared experiences.

As the sun began to set, casting a golden hue across the garden, we knew it was time to leave our secret oasis and return to the outside world. But in our hearts, the memories of that magical garden would forever be etched.

Together, we closed the gate and bid farewell to our hidden haven, knowing that we would return to tend to its growth and nourishment. Our shared adventure in the garden had strengthened our bond, instilling in us a deeper appreciation for nature, friendship, and the beauty of simple pleasures.

Little did we know that the hidden garden would be the backdrop to countless more adventures, serving as a constant reminder of the resilience, beauty, and growth that could emerge from even the most unexpected places..

Chapter 3

The day dawned with an air of excitement and anticipation. Thatelo and I had concocted a plan for an adventurous expedition, a journey to explore the nearby construction area with its small mountains of sand. The allure of the unknown beckoned us, and we couldn't resist the call.

We exchanged mischievous glances as we gathered our backpacks, filled with a sense of youthful curiosity and the tools we thought we might need for our exploration. Thatelo's eyes sparkled with excitement, her spirit matching mine in its eagerness to embark on this grand adventure. We knew it would be a day to remember, a day that would solidify our bond as siblings and explorers.

But as we prepared to set off, we couldn't shake off the heavy feeling in our hearts. Our beloved sister Noni, who had been ailing for some time, lay on the bed, her body weakened by an unknown illness. We knew the risks of leaving her behind, but the allure of the unknown was too strong to resist.

We hesitated for a moment, torn between our desire for adventure and our love for Noni. With heavy hearts, we made the difficult decision to proceed with our expedition, promising ourselves that we would return as swiftly as possible.

The construction area stood before us, a world of towering sand mountains and raw building materials. As we approached, our steps became lighter, our worries momentarily forgotten in the face of this new terrain. We marveled at the vastness of the sand, its grains glistening in the sunlight, beckoning us to explore further.

Hours turned into minutes as time seemed to slip away in the embrace of our makeshift playground. We climbed the sand mountains, feeling the grit between our fingers and toes. We built sandcastles, sculpting intricate designs with our hands. Laughter filled the air as we raced down the slopes, the sand spraying behind us.

But even in the midst of our adventure, a shadow lingered in the depths of our thoughts. We couldn't shake off the nagging worry for Noni, the fear that we had left her in a vulnerable state. As the sun began its descent, casting long shadows over the construction site, a sense of urgency washed over us.

With our hearts pounding, we retraced our steps, racing against time to reach home. The once-exciting expedition now felt like a burden, each step heavy with worry and guilt. We prayed silently for Noni's well-being, desperately hoping that we had made the right decision.

As we approached the familiar sight of our home, our footsteps faltered. The atmosphere seemed eerily still, as if the world held its breath. Dread gripped our hearts as we entered the house, our eyes searching for any signs of hope.

But what we found shattered our world.

Noni lay motionless on the bed, her face peaceful in eternal slumber. The disease that had plagued her had stolen her away in our absence. Shock and grief washed over us, leaving us stunned and inconsolable. Our once-vibrant sister, the pillar of strength in our lives, was now gone.

Tears streamed down our faces as we clung to each other, seeking solace in our shared pain. We were overwhelmed by a sense of loss, a realization of the fragility of life and the weight of our choices. The guilt weighed heavy on our young shoulders, a burden we would carry for years to come.

In that moment, the allure of adventure lost its luster. We had paid a heavy price for our exploration, a price that could never be reversed. We vowed never to let our youthful recklessness cloud our judgment again, to cherish and protect those we held dear.

As we mourned the loss of Noni, our expedition became a haunting memory, forever intertwined with sorrow and regret. We didn't have a chance to digest the magnitude of our loss before our parents arrived home.

Their footsteps echoed through the house, their voices filled with anticipation to see their children once again. But as they entered Noni's room, their joyful expressions turned to horror. Their cries pierced the air, the sound of their anguish reverberating through the walls.

"Mohlolo! Thatelo!" our mother's voice trembled with pain. "What has happened? How could you leave your sister when she needed you most?"

The weight of their sorrow crashed upon us, suffocating us in a sea of guilt. We had failed our sister, our family, and ourselves. Our parents' grief consumed us, their cries etching deep scars in our hearts.

We stood frozen, unable to find words to justify our actions. The tears streamed down our faces as we tried to convey our love, our remorse, and our deepest apologies. But no amount of remorse could turn back time or undo the irreversible loss we had suffered.

In that moment, our parents' pain became our pain, their sorrow became our burden to bear. We embraced each other, seeking solace and strength in our shared grief. We knew we had a long journey of healing ahead, one that would require forgiveness, understanding, and the unwavering love that bound us as a family.

Days turned into weeks, and weeks turned into months as we navigated the difficult path of grief together. Our parents' wounds slowly healed, but the scars remained, a constant reminder of the precious life we had lost. Noni's absence lingered in every corner of our home, an emptiness that could never be filled.

As we learned to cope with the pain, we also learned the importance of cherishing the moments we have with our loved ones. We understood the fragility of life and the need to seize every opportunity to show our love and support.

The memory of that tragic day etched itself into our souls, shaping us into more compassionate, responsible individuals. It served as a stark reminder of the consequences of our choices and the profound impact they could have on the lives of those we hold dear.

Our expedition to the construction site became a turning point in our lives, a catalyst for growth and introspection. We vowed to honor Noni's memory by living each day to the fullest, cherishing the gift of life and the precious bonds of family.

And as we looked ahead, our hearts heavy with grief but also filled with determination, we knew that our journey of healing had only just begun.

Chapter 4

In the aftermath of Noni's tragic passing, our once vibrant home was engulfed in an impenetrable cloud of sorrow. The weight of grief pressed down upon us, threatening to suffocate even the faintest glimmers of hope. It was during this time that we witnessed the devastating effects of depression on our parents.

The loss of Noni had shattered their hearts, leaving them fragmented and adrift in an abyss of despair. Each day became a battle, a struggle to find solace in a world that had become unbearably dark. My father, once a pillar of strength, succumbed to the overwhelming pain, losing his grip on reality.

His laughter was replaced by haunting silence, his eyes vacant and distant. He wandered aimlessly through the house, his once steady hands trembling with anxiety. The weight of guilt and sorrow consumed him, transforming him into a mere shadow of the man he used to be.

My mother, too, bore the heavy burden of grief. Her once vibrant spirit had dimmed, replaced by a constant state of anguish. She withdrew from the world, retreating into the depths of her sorrow. The walls of our home echoed with her tears, a symphony of pain that pierced our hearts.

As their children, we were helpless witnesses to their torment. We longed to ease their suffering, to bring back the light that had been extinguished from their eyes. But grief is a labyrinth with no easy way out, and we were all lost within its tangled corridors.

Days turned into weeks, and weeks turned into months, yet the darkness persisted. We watched helplessly as our parents grappled with their demons, their once strong spirits crumbling beneath the weight of their despair. The anguish carved lines upon their faces, etching a painful story of loss and sorrow.

In the depths of their despair, our parents clung to each other, finding solace in their shared pain. They sought therapy and support, reaching out for a lifeline to guide them through the darkness. It was a slow and arduous journey, but they were determined to find healing, not only for themselves but for the sake of our family.

Through therapy and counseling, they began to piece together the fragments of their shattered hearts. They learned to lean on each other, finding strength in their shared grief. Slowly, ever so slowly, small rays of hope began to pierce through the darkness that had enveloped our home.

While the wounds of loss remained, our parents embarked on a path of healing. They sought ways to honor Noni's memory, to keep her spirit alive within us. They started a foundation in her name, dedicated to raising awareness about mental health and supporting families who had experienced similar tragedies.

As we witnessed their journey from the depths of despair to a place of resilience, we learned the power of love, support, and the indomitable human spirit. Our parents' battle with depression taught us the importance of reaching out, of seeking help when we need it most.

In the face of adversity, we discovered our own strength. We became a family united in our shared grief, bound by a fierce determination to heal and to honor the memory of our beloved Noni.

And as we stepped into the next chapter of our lives, we carried with us the lessons learned from the darkness. We embraced the fragile beauty of life, cherishing every precious moment and finding solace in the resilience of the human spirit.

Chapter 5

In the aftermath of Noni's tragic passing, our once vibrant home was engulfed in an impenetrable cloud of sorrow. The weight of grief pressed down upon us, threatening to suffocate even the faintest glimmers of hope. It was during this time that we witnessed the devastating effects of depression on our parents.

The loss of Noni had shattered their hearts, leaving them fragmented and adrift in an abyss of despair. Each day became a battle, a struggle to find solace in a world that had become unbearably dark. My father, once a pillar of strength, succumbed to the overwhelming pain, losing his grip on reality.

His laughter was replaced by haunting silence, his eyes vacant and distant. He wandered aimlessly through the house, his once steady hands trembling with anxiety. The weight of guilt and sorrow consumed him, transforming him into a mere shadow of the man he used to be.

My mother, too, bore the heavy burden of grief. Her once vibrant spirit had dimmed, replaced by a constant state of anguish. She withdrew from the world, retreating into the depths of her sorrow. The walls of our home echoed with her tears, a symphony of pain that pierced our hearts.

As their children, we were helpless witnesses to their torment. We longed to ease their suffering, to bring back the light that had been extinguished from their eyes. But grief is a labyrinth with no easy way out, and we were all lost within its tangled corridors.

Days turned into weeks, and weeks turned into months, yet the darkness persisted. We watched helplessly as our parents grappled with their demons, their once strong spirits crumbling beneath the weight of their despair. The anguish carved lines upon their faces, etching a painful story of loss and sorrow.

In the depths of their despair, our parents clung to each other, finding solace in their shared pain. They sought therapy and support, reaching out for a lifeline to guide them through the darkness. It was a slow and arduous journey, but they were determined to find healing, not only for themselves but for the sake of our family.

Through therapy and counseling, they began to piece together the fragments of their shattered hearts. They learned to lean on each other, finding strength in their shared grief. Slowly, ever so slowly, small rays of hope began to pierce through the darkness that had enveloped our home.

While the wounds of loss remained, our parents embarked on a path of healing. They sought ways to honor Noni's memory, to keep her spirit alive within us. They started a foundation in her name, dedicated to raising awareness about mental health and supporting families who had experienced similar tragedies.

As we witnessed their journey from the depths of despair to a place of resilience, we learned the power of love, support, and the indomitable human spirit. Our parents' battle with depression taught us the importance of reaching out, of seeking help when we need it most.

In the face of adversity, we discovered our own strength. We became a family united in our shared grief, bound by a fierce determination to heal and to honor the memory of our beloved Noni.

And as we stepped into the next chapter of our lives, we carried with us the lessons learned from the darkness. We embraced the fragile beauty of life, cherishing every precious moment and finding solace in the resilience of the human spirit.

Chapter 6

Within the walls of the St. Louis Children's Home, a beacon of hope emerged in the form of MaMokoena. She was the heart and soul of the home, a woman whose warmth and compassion touched the lives of every child who crossed her path. As the cook of the home, she nourished our bodies with her delicious meals, but it was her nurturing spirit that truly fed our souls.

MaMokoena took a special interest in our story, sensing the depth of our pain and longing. She saw beyond the scars that grief had etched into our young hearts and recognized the resilience that lay within us. From the moment we arrived at the home, she became our pillar of support, a mother figure who offered solace and unconditional love.

Every week, MaMokoena sat down with us and helped us write heartfelt letters to our late mother. With her guidance, we poured our emotions onto the pages, sharing our joys, our sorrows, and our dreams. Through the act of writing, we found a way to connect with our mother's spirit, to keep her memory alive in our hearts.

But MaMokoena's love extended far beyond the confines of the written word. She embraced us with open arms, offering hugs that felt like a warm embrace from a long-lost relative. In her presence, we found a safe haven, a place where we could shed our masks of strength and vulnerability. She listened to our stories, our fears, and our dreams, offering words of wisdom and encouragement.

As the days turned into weeks and the weeks into months, MaMokoena's love and guidance became an anchor in our lives. She taught us valuable life lessons, instilling in us the importance of resilience, kindness, and self-belief. Through her nurturing spirit, we began to heal, slowly but surely, from the wounds of our past.

The aroma of MaMokoena's cooking filled the air, serving as a constant reminder of her love and care. She created meals that not only nourished our bodies but also fed our souls. Each dish was prepared with meticulous attention to detail, infused with flavors that brought comfort and a sense of home. The dining table became a place of warmth and laughter, where we shared meals and stories with our newfound family at the children's home.

In the evenings, as we gathered around the communal area, MaMokoena would regale us with tales of hope and resilience. Her stories ignited our imaginations, transporting us to worlds of wonder and possibility. Through her words, we learned that adversity could be overcome, and that dreams could blossom even in the most challenging circumstances.

It was during one such evening that MaMokoena shared a story of triumph against all odds. She spoke of a young girl who defied expectations and pursued her passion for art. The tale resonated deeply within us, igniting a spark of inspiration and the desire to explore our own creative potential.

With MaMokoena's unwavering support and encouragement, we began to nurture our artistic inclinations. She provided us with art supplies, encouraged us to express ourselves through various mediums, and celebrated our creations with genuine delight. In her eyes, we saw a reflection of our own potential, and we felt a growing sense of purpose.

As the days unfolded, we realized that MaMokoena had become more than just a cook or a caretaker. She had become our mother in every sense of the word. Her presence filled the void that resided deep within our hearts, bringing us a sense of belonging and security. She became the guiding light that illuminated our path forward, helping us navigate the complexities of life with grace and resilience.

Under MaMokoena's loving guidance, we flourished at the St. Louis Children's Home. She encouraged our artistic endeavors, providing us with the space and resources to explore our creativity. With her by our side, we delved into the world of art, discovering new techniques, experimenting with colors, and allowing our imaginations to run wild on the canvas.

MaMokoena's unwavering belief in our abilities propelled us to new heights. She nurtured our talents, recognizing the unique gifts we possessed. She saw the potential within us and fostered an environment where we could grow and develop into the individuals we were meant to be.

Beyond our artistic pursuits, MaMokoena taught us important life skills and values. She instilled in us a strong work ethic, teaching us the importance of dedication and perseverance. She encouraged us to pursue our dreams, reminding us that with determination and hard work, anything was possible.

But it was not just her practical teachings that left an indelible mark on our lives. It was the way she embraced us with her love, offering a safe space where we could be vulnerable and express our emotions. In her comforting presence, we found solace and the courage to face the pain that lingered within us.

And as we embarked on the next chapter of our lives, we carried MaMokoena's love and teachings in our hearts.

Chapter 7

The day came when Thatelo received the life-altering news that a family had chosen to adopt her. Excitement danced in her eyes, but as she processed the information, a cloud of sadness veiled her joy. She couldn't fathom leaving me behind, her brother and confidant, who had been her constant companion in the face of adversity.

Her heart conflicted, Thatelo approached me with a heavy heart. We sat under the shade of the old oak tree near our beloved St. Louis Children's Home, seeking solace in the familiar surroundings that had shaped us. Tears welled in her eyes as she mustered the strength to share her internal struggle.

"Mohlolo," she whispered, her voice filled with anguish, "I've been chosen for adoption. A family wants to give me a home, but I can't bear to leave you behind. We've faced so much together, and the thought of being separated is unbearable."

The weight of her words sank deep into my soul. I understood her fear, her longing for stability, and the torment of choosing between a family's love and our unbreakable bond. In that moment, my heart ached, knowing that our paths might diverge, even if temporarily.

With a tender gaze, I reached out and took Thatelo's trembling hand. "You deserve this chance, Thatelo," I said softly, my voice filled with reassurance. "Family isn't just about being physically together. No matter where life takes us, you will always be in my heart, and I in yours. We'll find a way to stay connected, even if our circumstances change."

Reluctantly, Thatelo agreed to embark on this new chapter of her life, to seize the opportunity that awaited her. With a heavy heart, she bid farewell to our St. Louis Children's Home and the memories it held.

We clung to each other, tears staining our cheeks, as she embarked on a journey into the unknown.

Days turned into weeks, and weeks into months. Thatelo settled into her new home, the embrace of her adoptive family. Yet, the void left in my life by her absence echoed loudly. Though we exchanged letters and spoke on the phone, our conversations were bittersweet reminders of the physical distance between us.

But destiny had its own plans. Thatelo, despite the comforts of her new life, couldn't silence the voice within her that yearned to be reunited with me, her brother. The pull of our bond was too strong to ignore. And so, she made the courageous decision to escape back to St. Louis, to the place where our shared journey began.

Late one moonlit night, as the world slumbered, Thatelo slipped away from the safety of her adoptive home. With determination fueling her every step, she navigated the unfamiliar streets, retracing the path that had once led her away from me. The city's silent alleys whispered stories of her unwavering love and her unyielding spirit.

When Thatelo arrived at our cherished St. Louis Children's Home, she sought solace in the familiar embrace of our old room. Memories flooded her senses, reminding her of the unconditional support and understanding we had found within those walls. It was a temporary respite, a sanctuary where she could gather her thoughts and emotions.

Meanwhile, the news of Thatelo's escape reached me. My heart swelled with a mix of worry and hope. I knew the depth of her determination, but I also recognized the complexities of her situation. I couldn't bear the thought of her facing the world alone, but I understood her need for independence and her longing to find her own path.

Guided by an unwavering

resolve, I made my way to St. Louis, where I found Thatelo, weary and uncertain. The reunion was both joyous and heart-wrenching, for we knew the decision that lay ahead. With tears streaming down our cheeks, we held each other tightly, knowing that we couldn't remain at the children's home indefinitely.

Together, we confronted the reality of our situation and the choices we had to make. We spent hours under the starlit sky, contemplating our futures, the weight of responsibility heavy upon us. In the end, we knew what we had to do. We had to convince Thatelo to return to her adoptive family, where she could continue the journey she had begun.

Through tearful conversations, heartfelt promises, and a shared understanding, we convinced Thatelo to embrace the love and opportunity her adoptive family offered. We vowed to never forget each other, to cherish the bond that time and distance could not erode. We promised to support each other from afar, to be each other's guiding light in times of darkness.

As Thatelo returned to her adoptive family, we clung to the hope that our paths would cross again someday. And though we faced an uncertain future, we knew that the love and connection we shared would endure. Our bond was forged through adversity, and it would stand the test of time.

And so, with heavy hearts and unyielding determination, we embarked on separate journeys, trusting that fate would one day reunite us. Thatelo carried my unwavering love within her, a constant reminder that we were never truly apart. Our story was not yet finished, and the chapters yet to be written held the promise of reunion and new beginnings.

Throughout our lives, we are faced with difficult choices and moments of separation. It is during these times that we discover the true strength of our bonds and the power of love. The experience of Thatelo's journey reminds us of the profound impact relationships can have on our lives.

The moral that resonates from this experience is the importance of cherishing and nurturing the connections we forge with others. Whether they are family, friends, or kindred spirits, these relationships shape our identity and provide us with strength, support, and guidance.

Life's path may lead us in different directions, and circumstances may separate us physically, but the ties that bind us remain unbroken. It is through love, understanding, and unwavering loyalty that we can weather the storms of separation and find solace in the knowledge that true connections endure.

In the face of adversity, we must hold onto the memories, the lessons, and the shared experiences that have shaped us. We must embrace the beauty of human connection and strive to cultivate meaningful relationships that enrich our lives.

As we navigate the complexities of life, let us remember the moral of this experience: to cherish those we hold dear, to treasure the bonds that transcend distance, and to embrace the power of love that unites us. For in the tapestry of our lives, it is the threads of connection that weave the most beautiful and enduring stories.

Chapter 8

MaMokoena had become more than just a cook to me; she was like a guardian angel, providing me with comfort, love, and guidance during my time at the St Louis Children's Home. Our bond grew stronger each day, and she began considering the idea of adopting me as her own. It was a prospect that filled me with both hope and uncertainty.

One day, MaMokoena sat me down at the kitchen table, her warm smile contrasting with the seriousness in her eyes. She gently held my hand, her touch comforting and reassuring.

"Mohlolo, my dear child," she began, her voice filled with tenderness. "I have been thinking a lot about our future together. The possibility of adopting you and becoming your mother has crossed my mind many times."

My heart skipped a beat as a surge of emotions rushed through me. The idea of having a loving family again, of belonging somewhere, was both exciting and overwhelming.

"But I need you to understand something, Mohlolo," she continued. "Adoption is not a decision to be taken lightly. It involves a lot of legal processes and considerations. I have applied to adopt you, but it may not be as easy as we hope."

As she spoke those words, I felt a pang of disappointment. The realization that our journey towards a new family might face obstacles was difficult to bear. Yet, MaMokoena's words also carried an underlying sense of understanding and empathy.

She took a moment to gather her thoughts before continuing. "I want you to know that, regardless of the outcome, you will always hold a special place in my heart. I am here for you, no matter what happens. We are family, Mohlolo, and nothing can change that."

Tears welled up in my eyes as I embraced her tightly. In that moment, I realized that family goes beyond legal documents and formalities. It is about the love, care, and support we offer one another.

Over the following weeks, MaMokoena and I would often sit together, reminiscing about my parents and the life we once had. She would listen attentively as I shared stories about my father's jokes and my mother's comforting presence. It was in those conversations that I found solace and healing.

MaMokoena understood the depths of my experience, the pain of loss, and the longing for a place to call home. She validated my emotions and provided me with a safe space to express my grief.

She would often say, "Mohlolo, your family may not be with you physically, but their love and spirit will always be with you. They would be so proud of the remarkable person you are becoming."

Her words resonated within me, filling me with a renewed sense of strength and resilience. Even if the adoption did not come to fruition, I knew that I had someone in my corner, someone who cared deeply for me.

Days turned into weeks, and weeks into months. The news finally arrived that MaMokoena's adoption application had been denied. It was a heartbreaking blow, but MaMokoena remained steadfast in her commitment to me.

With tears in her eyes, she held my hands and whispered, "Mohlolo, my dear, this may not be the outcome we hoped for, but please know that you are loved, cherished, and always welcome in my heart and home. We will navigate this journey together, side by side."

In that moment, I understood the true meaning of family. It was not bound by legalities or official titles, but by the deep connections and unwavering support we share with those who genuinely care for us.

MaMokoena's love and understanding had become my guiding

light, illuminating the path ahead. Although the road to finding my place in the world was filled with challenges, I knew that I was not alone.

And with MaMokoena by my side, I felt a renewed sense of hope and determination to create a future filled with love and belonging.

Together, we would navigate the complexities of life, supporting one another, and cherishing the bond that had formed between us. As we faced the uncertainties that lay ahead, I knew that with MaMokoena's love and guidance, I would always find my way.

Chapter 9

As I stepped into the gates of Taiwe Secondary School, a new chapter of my life began. It was a bustling place, filled with students from different backgrounds, each with their own dreams and aspirations. Little did I know that within those walls, I would forge a friendship that would change the course of my life.

Lebohang, the daughter of a dedicated policeman, was a ray of sunshine amidst the academic challenges and social dynamics of high school. With her infectious laughter and unwavering determination, she quickly became my closest companion. We were two peas in a pod, navigating the intricate maze of teenagehood together.

It was during our first year at Taiwe Secondary School that Ms. Khosana, our passionate English teacher, introduced us to the world of public speaking. She believed that the power of words had the ability to transform lives and ignite change. Ms. Khosana encouraged us to participate in a school-wide public speaking competition, an opportunity to showcase our voices and unleash our potential.

The idea both excited and terrified me. As someone who had always been reserved and hesitant to speak in public, the thought of standing in front of an audience filled me with dread. But Lebohang, with her unwavering support and belief in my abilities, convinced me to give it a try.

We spent countless afternoons practicing our speeches, encouraging each other to find our voices and speak our truths. Lebohang's confidence was contagious, and her words of encouragement fueled my determination. Together, we delved into the depths of our experiences, weaving our stories into powerful narratives that would captivate the hearts and minds of our listeners.

The day of the competition arrived, and my nerves threatened to overwhelm me. As I stood in front of the sea of faces, my voice trembled, and my palms grew sweaty. The words I had practiced so diligently seemed to escape me, and I stumbled through my speech, unable to convey the message I had so passionately prepared.

Disheartened, I considered giving up. But it was Lebohang's unwavering support that kept me going. She reminded me of my potential, of the unique perspective I brought to the stage. With her by my side, I found the courage to persevere, to dust myself off, and try again.

Lebohang became my anchor, offering guidance and mentorship. She shared her own experiences of failure and reminded me that setbacks were not the end of the road, but rather opportunities for growth. Together, we rewrote and refined our speeches, honing our skills and harnessing the power of our voices.

In Grade 8, I returned to the public speaking competition with newfound determination. This time, as I stood before the audience, I spoke with conviction, pouring my heart into every word. The room became still, and a wave of resonance filled the air. The audience listened intently, captivated by the passion in my voice and the authenticity of my message.

When I finished, the room erupted into applause. It was a standing ovation, a testament to the growth I had achieved and the power of perseverance. As I looked out into the crowd, my eyes met Lebohang's, and I saw pride and joy reflected in her gaze.

That day marked a turning point in my life. Through Lebohang's unwavering support and our shared journey of growth, I discovered the strength within me to overcome my fears and embrace the power of my voice. Public speaking became not just a competition, but a tool through which I could inspire, educate, and connect with others.

Lebohang's friendship became an anchor in my life, a reminder that true friends believe in our potential even when we doubt ourselves. Together

, we continued to explore the realms of public speaking, honing our skills and pushing each other to new heights.

Little did I know that this experience would set the stage for the adventures and challenges that lay ahead. As I embarked on my high school journey, I carried with me the lessons learned from Taiwe Secondary School, the power of friendship, and the belief that with the right companions by my side, anything was possible.

Chapter 10

As the years passed at Taiwe Secondary School, my friendship with Lebohang blossomed into something deeper. We shared laughter, tears, and countless moments of vulnerability. But amidst the warmth and comfort of our connection, a new emotion began to stir within me—a feeling I couldn't quite comprehend.

It was during a sunny afternoon in Grade 11, as we sat together under the shade of a tall tree in the schoolyard, that a surge of courage compelled me to lean in and kiss Lebohang. In that fleeting moment, time stood still, and I felt a rush of emotions intertwining within me—anticipation, fear, and a flicker of something more profound.

But as our lips parted and reality rushed back in, an overwhelming sense of guilt washed over me. What had I done? Had I risked our friendship by succumbing to these confusing emotions? I feared that I had crossed a line, jeopardizing the bond we had nurtured over the years.

In the days that followed, I grappled with a whirlwind of emotions—regret, confusion, and a deep longing for things to return to the way they were before that fateful kiss. I questioned my actions, doubting my intentions and the consequences they might have on our friendship.

Unable to bear the weight of my guilt any longer, I approached Lebohang one afternoon during our lunch break. We found solace in our usual spot under the tree, but this time, the atmosphere felt heavy with unspoken words. I mustered the courage to open up, to share the turmoil within my heart.

Tears welled up in my eyes as I confessed my fear of losing her, of allowing my tangled emotions to taint the beautiful friendship we had built. Lebohang listened with empathy, her eyes reflecting understanding and compassion. She reassured me that our bond was strong enough to weather this storm, that our friendship could withstand the complexity of feelings.

In that moment, a profound sense of relief washed over me. Lebohang's acceptance and unwavering support reminded me of the strength and resilience of our connection. We both acknowledged the depth of our emotions, the significance of that kiss, but we also recognized that it didn't have to define us.

From that day forward, we embarked on a journey of self-discovery, navigating the intricacies of our friendship with newfound clarity. We set boundaries and communicated openly about our feelings, ensuring that our connection remained grounded in trust and understanding.

While the path wasn't always smooth, our friendship grew stronger through our shared vulnerability and commitment to preserving what we cherished most. We embraced the complexity of our feelings, acknowledging that they were an inherent part of being human, but never allowing them to overshadow the deep-rooted friendship we had cultivated.

Looking back, I realized that our kiss had served as a catalyst for growth and introspection. It allowed us to delve deeper into ourselves, exploring the intricacies of our emotions and the power they held over our lives. It taught me that forgiveness, both for oneself and others, is an essential ingredient in maintaining strong and enduring relationships.

In the end, our friendship flourished, not in spite of that kiss, but because we confronted it head-on and learned from it. We continued to support each other's dreams, uplift one another, and face the challenges of high school and beyond, hand in hand.

Through this experience, I discovered the importance of honesty, vulnerability, and the unwavering power of friendship. Our journey together had taught me that true connections could weather storms and emerge stronger, that forgiveness and understanding were essential ingredients in building lasting bonds.

As we navigated the final years of our high school journey, I carried the memory of that kiss as a reminder that love, in all its complexities, can coexist with friendship. It taught me that the boundaries of our relationships are not set in stone but can evolve and expand as we navigate the depths of our emotions.

Lebohang and I became each other's pillars of strength, supporting one another through the highs and lows of our teenage years. We celebrated each other's successes, consoled each other in moments of disappointment, and encouraged one another to chase our dreams fearlessly.

But even as our bond deepened, I couldn't shake the nagging feeling of guilt that still lingered within me. Despite Lebohang's understanding and forgiveness, I struggled to forgive myself fully for jeopardizing our friendship. The weight of my perceived mistake weighed heavily on my heart.

It wasn't until one evening, as the sun dipped below the horizon and painted the sky with hues of orange and pink, that I found solace in a heartfelt conversation with Lebohang. We sat on a park bench, our shoulders touching, as we bared our souls to one another.

Lebohang's words resonated deeply within me. She spoke of forgiveness not only for others but also for ourselves. She reminded me that we are all flawed beings, prone to making mistakes, but it is through forgiveness and self-compassion that we can find healing and growth.

In that vulnerable moment, I made a choice to let go of the burden I had carried for so long. I forgave myself for the kiss, recognizing that it was an expression of genuine emotions and not something to be condemned or regretted. It was a part of my journey, a stepping stone towards self-discovery.

From that point forward, our friendship thrived even more. We continued to support and uplift one another, creating cherished memories and shared experiences. We embarked on new adventures, pursued our passions, and faced the challenges of life with unwavering support.

As we stood side by side on the cusp of our high school graduation, I looked back on our journey with gratitude. The kiss that once haunted me had become a catalyst for personal growth and a testament to the resilience of our friendship. It was a reminder that mistakes do not define us; it is how we respond and learn from them that shapes our character.

Lebohang and I vowed to carry the lessons we had learned throughout our lives. We understood the power of forgiveness, the value of honesty, and the importance of embracing the complexities of our emotions. Together, we had navigated the intricacies of friendship and emerged stronger and wiser.

In the tapestry of our lives, that kiss remained a thread that wove us together, a symbol of our shared journey through adolescence. It served as a reminder that even in the face of uncertainty and mistakes, true friendship could prevail, and love could thrive.

And so, with our hearts filled with gratitude and anticipation for the future, we embraced the next chapter of our lives, knowing that no matter where our paths led us, the foundation of our friendship would forever be unwavering.

Chapter 12

As Grade 9 began, Lebohang and I found ourselves stepping onto a bigger stage. We were no longer the newbies, but rather the older students in the school. It was during this time that an exciting opportunity presented itself—an art competition where each Grade 9 class would showcase their creative talents. Little did we know that this event would become a turning point in our journey.

The theme for the competition was "Icons of Change," and each class had to choose a prominent figure who had made a significant impact on society. Our class teacher, Ms. Khosana, encouraged us to think beyond the obvious choices and delve into the lives of lesser-known heroes. After much deliberation, we unanimously agreed to celebrate the life and legacy of Nelson Mandela, the iconic leader who fought tirelessly for freedom and equality in our country.

The days leading up to the competition were filled with intense preparations. Lebohang and I spent countless hours researching, brainstorming ideas, and practicing our speeches. We wanted to capture the essence of Mandela's spirit, his resilience, and his unwavering belief in the power of unity. Our goal was to inspire our classmates and the entire school through our presentation.

The day of the competition arrived, and the atmosphere in the school hall was buzzing with anticipation. Each Grade 9 class showcased their creative expressions of change, from visual art installations to powerful poetry performances. Finally, it was our turn to take the stage.

As I stood before the microphone, my heart pounded with nervous excitement. Lebohang and I had rehearsed our parts meticulously, but there was always an element of uncertainty when facing a large audience. However, as I began speaking, a sense of calm washed over me. I channeled the strength and courage of Nelson Mandela, allowing his words to flow through me.

With each sentence, I painted a vivid picture of Mandela's life, highlighting his struggles, sacrifices, and ultimate triumph. Lebohang, standing beside me, complemented my words with a mesmerizing interpretive dance, capturing the emotions and essence of Mandela's journey. Together, we created a powerful synergy that captivated the audience.

In that moment, I felt a surge of confidence and purpose. The words flowed effortlessly, as if guided by an unseen force. I found myself imitating Mandela's distinctive voice, his gestures, and even his contagious smile. The audience responded with thunderous applause, their energy fueling our performance.

When we finished, the hall erupted in cheers and accolades. The judges praised our unique approach and the emotional impact of our presentation. It was a moment of validation, not just for our artistic abilities, but also for the deep connection we had forged with Mandela's message of unity and forgiveness.

That day marked a turning point in our lives. It was not just about winning the competition but discovering the power of our voices, the ability to inspire change through art and storytelling. From that moment forward, Lebohang and I realized the potential within us to make a difference, no matter how small.

As we left the stage that day, hand in hand, we knew our journey was just beginning. The path ahead would be filled with more challenges, triumphs, and opportunities to use our voices for good. With Lebohang by my side, I felt unstoppable, ready to face whatever came our way.

Little did we know that the next chapter of our lives would take us on even greater adventures, shaping us into the individuals we were meant to become. The legacy of Nelson Mandela would continue to inspire us, reminding us that change starts with a single voice—and ours was just getting started.

Chapter 13

Life has a way of taking us down unexpected paths, and as we entered Grade 10, Lebohang's journey took a different turn. She received an opportunity to transfer to a renowned ex-Model C school, known for its academic excellence and vast opportunities. It was a chance for her to broaden her horizons and explore new avenues of growth.

As Lebohang shared the news with me, a mix of emotions washed over me. I was undeniably proud of her, knowing that she deserved every opportunity that came her way. At the same time, a sense of sadness crept into my heart, realizing that our paths would now diverge.

Lebohang understood my mixed feelings and wanted to leave a lasting memento of our friendship. On the day before her departure, she handed me a small gift wrapped in vibrant paper. With a bittersweet smile, she told me to open it when I missed her the most.

Curiosity tingled within me as I carefully unwrapped the gift. Inside was a beautifully crafted journal with a personalized message on the first page. Lebohang's words danced across the paper, expressing her gratitude for our friendship and the profound impact it had on her life.

She encouraged me to continue writing, to pour my thoughts and emotions onto the pages, just as we had done during our adventures in storytelling and public speaking. The journal was a symbol of our shared dreams, a reminder that even when physically apart, our hearts would remain connected through the power of words.

As I held the journal in my hands, a surge of gratitude washed over me. Lebohang's gift was not just a token of remembrance; it was a testament to the bond we had formed, the lessons we had learned, and the dreams we had shared. It was a reminder that true friendship transcends distance and time.

In the following days, Lebohang bid farewell to our school, leaving behind a void that could never be fully filled. But her presence lingered in the halls, in the memories we had created, and in the dreams we had nurtured together.

I kept the journal close to my heart, using it as a sanctuary for my thoughts, aspirations, and reflections. Whenever I missed Lebohang, I would open its pages and find solace in the words we had exchanged, the dreams we had dared to chase.

Life moved on, and our paths continued to unfold in different directions. Yet, the gift of Lebohang's friendship remained a guiding light, igniting a spark of inspiration within me. I knew that our journey was far from over and that the memories we had shared would forever shape the person I was becoming.

As I turned the pages of the journal, I realized that true friendships are not bound by time or distance. They are woven into the fabric of our lives, etching their mark on our souls. Lebohang had left an indelible impression on my heart, and her gift would forever serve as a reminder of the transformative power of friendship.

With renewed determination and a heart full of gratitude, I embarked on the next chapter of my life, ready to embrace new experiences, forge new connections, and honor the bond Lebohang and I had shared. Little did I know that the universe had more surprises in store for me, weaving together the threads of destiny to lead me towards my purpose.

And so, I set forth, carrying Lebohang's gift of friendship as a cherished treasure, knowing that no matter where our paths may lead, the memories we had created would forever guide me on my journey of self-discovery and growth.

Chapter 14

The final year of high school, the pinnacle of our educational journey, arrived with a mix of anticipation and trepidation. It was the year that would shape our futures, the year of matriculation. As we stood on the threshold of this defining chapter, we were determined to give it our all.

In an effort to create an immersive and focused study environment, our school made a unique arrangement for us. Instead of the traditional camping trip, we were given the opportunity to sleep on the stage of our school's grand exam hall. It was an unconventional choice, but it allowed us to be in close proximity to our study materials and each other, fostering an atmosphere of collaboration and support.

The exam hall, typically a space filled with nervous energy and anticipation during exams, became our temporary abode. We set up makeshift sleeping areas with blankets and pillows, transforming the stage into a dormitory. It was a symbol of our dedication, a constant reminder of the goal we were striving towards.

The days melded into nights as we immersed ourselves in the world of textbooks, revision guides, and past exam papers. We formed study groups, huddled together under the dim lights, sharing our knowledge, doubts, and triumphs. The stage became our haven, a sanctuary of focused learning and camaraderie.

As night fell, the exam hall came alive with the soft glow of desk lamps illuminating our diligent faces. The sound of pages turning and pens scratching filled the air. We exchanged study tips, reviewed challenging concepts, and pushed one another to reach new heights of understanding.

Sleepless nights became the norm, but we were fueled by a collective drive to excel. The weight of expectations bore down on our shoulders, but we persevered, reminding ourselves of the importance of this final stretch. We sought solace in the companionship of our fellow students, sharing laughter, encouragement, and the occasional midnight snack.

During breaks, we would explore the quiet corridors of the school, seeking moments of respite from the intensity of our studies. We would find solace in the empty classrooms, contemplating the knowledge imparted within their walls. The school became our sanctuary, a testament to our years of growth and the memories we had created.

As the days turned into weeks and the weeks into months, the exams loomed ever closer. The pressure was palpable, but we remained steadfast. We attended extra classes, sought guidance from our teachers, and delved into the depths of our chosen subjects. The stage on which we slept also became the stage where we performed, where we showcased our knowledge and skills.

The day of the final exam finally arrived, and the exam hall buzzed with nervous energy. We took our seats, our minds focused and hearts racing. The room fell silent as we turned over the exam papers, each question beckoning us to showcase our understanding and mastery.

Time seemed to both stand still and race forward as we poured our thoughts onto the pages before us. We wrote with conviction, our pens dancing across the paper, articulating the knowledge and insights we had acquired over the years. In those moments, we were not merely students taking an exam; we were scholars, ready to leave our mark on the world.

As the final minutes ticked away, we completed our last sentences and handed in our papers. A wave of relief washed over us, accompanied by a sense of accomplishment. We had done it. We had persevered through sleepless nights, endless revisions, and moments of doubt. We had risen to the challenge and conquered the exams that had once seemed insurmountable.

As we left the exam hall, our steps lighter and hearts full, we carried with us the lessons learned, the friendships forged, and the indomitable spirit that pulsated within us. The matric year had been a transformative experience, a culmination of years of hard work and dedication. It was a chapter that would forever be etched in our memories, shaping the trajectory of our lives.

But beyond the academic accomplishments, the stage on which we had slept held a deeper significance. It symbolized the unity and resilience of our class, the unwavering support we had provided one another throughout the journey. We had transformed a space meant for examinations into a haven of collaboration, where friendships blossomed and bonds grew stronger.

As we stepped out into the world beyond the school's walls, we carried the lessons learned during our matric year. We had learned the value of discipline, perseverance, and the power of collective effort. We had discovered the importance of balance, knowing when to study, when to rest, and when to find solace in the company of friends.

But above all, we had realized that success was not solely measured by grades and academic achievements. It encompassed personal growth, resilience, and the ability to navigate the challenges that life would inevitably present. The stage on which we had slept had become a metaphor for our journey—a reminder that sometimes we must step outside our comfort zones, embrace unconventional approaches, and find strength in unity.

As we bid farewell to our beloved school and the exam hall that had become our sanctuary, we knew that the memories created within those walls would forever hold a special place in our hearts. We were now ready to embark on the next phase of our lives, armed with the knowledge that we could conquer any obstacle that stood in our way.

But as we left, we promised ourselves and each other that we would never forget the experiences we had shared. We vowed to carry the camaraderie and support we had fostered into the future, ensuring that the lessons learned during our matric year would guide us in our pursuits and shape us into compassionate, resilient individuals.

The stage on which we had slept during our matric year would remain a symbol of our determination, our unwavering spirit, and the memories we had forged. It would serve as a reminder of the friendships we had cultivated, the challenges we had overcome, and the dreams we had dared to pursue.

And so, with hearts full of gratitude and minds brimming with ambition, we bid farewell to the stage that had witnessed our transformation. We took one last look back, knowing that it was not just a physical space but a testament to the incredible journey we had embarked upon together.

The stage may have been left behind, but the lessons learned and the bonds forged during our matric year would forever illuminate our paths. We were ready to face the world, armed with knowledge, resilience, and the unwavering support of our fellow classmates. The stage may have been our temporary home, but the memories and experiences it held would forever shape our futures.

Chapter 15

Leaving St Louis Children's Home marked the end of a significant chapter in my life. It was a bittersweet transition, saying goodbye to the familiar faces and routines that had shaped my days. But as I ventured into the next phase of my journey, I was filled with anticipation and a sense of newfound independence.

My destination was not a grand mansion or a luxurious estate, but a humble abode where I would start anew. MaMokoena, the kind-hearted soul who had touched my life in countless ways, welcomed me into her home with open arms. The small dwelling became my haven, a place where I could rebuild and rediscover myself.

As I settled into my new surroundings, a wave of emotions washed over me. The quietude of the space offered solace, and the absence of other children reminded me that this was a fresh beginning, a chance to find my own path. MaMokoena's presence brought comfort and reassurance, as she became more than just a caretaker—she became the family I had longed for.

In this new home, I learned the true meaning of solitude and self-discovery. The walls echoed with the stories of my past, and the silence allowed me to reflect on my journey and envision the possibilities that lay ahead. The aroma of MaMokoena's cooking filled the air, enveloping me in a sense of warmth and belonging.

As the days turned into weeks and the weeks into months, I began to find my place within this newfound independence. MaMokoena's guidance and unwavering support became my guiding light, offering me the tools and encouragement to navigate the challenges that lay before me. Her wisdom became the compass that pointed me in the right direction as I sought to create a future filled with purpose and fulfillment.

Living alone with MaMokoena allowed me to embrace my individuality and explore my passions without the distractions of sibling dynamics. I delved into my studies, devoting myself to academic excellence and personal growth. MaMokoena's home became a sanctuary where I could pursue my dreams and aspirations, free from the constraints that had once held me back.

However, as I pondered my future, I found myself unsure of the career path I had once envisioned. The desire to become a teacher, which had burned passionately within me, was now tinged with uncertainty. I questioned whether it was still the right path for me, and this uncertainty led me to make a difficult decision.

Instead of immediately applying for university, I decided to take a gap year—a year to explore, learn, and gain clarity about my aspirations. It was a bold choice, one that allowed me the freedom to step back and evaluate my true passions and goals.

During my gap year, I engaged in various activities that broadened my horizons. I volunteered at local organizations, traveled to different places, and pursued hobbies that sparked my curiosity. I immersed myself in new experiences, eager to discover what truly ignited my soul.

MaMokoena, always a source of wisdom and support, encouraged me to use this time to reflect on my dreams and aspirations. She reminded me that the path to finding my purpose might be winding and uncertain, but as long as I remained true to myself, I would eventually uncover it.

As the days turned into months, and my gap year came to a close, I found myself transformed. The experiences and self-reflection had led me to a renewed sense of purpose. While I had once doubted my path, I now knew with conviction that my passion lay in entrepreneurship and business.

With a newfound clarity, I prepared to embark on the next chapter of my life—university studies focused on business and entrepreneurship. The gap year had provided me with the necessary perspective and self-discovery to confidently pursue this new direction. I felt a surge of excitement and determination as I prepared my applications and researched the best universities to nurture my entrepreneurial ambitions.

During this time, MaMokoena continued to be my pillar of strength and guidance. She listened attentively to my aspirations, offering words of encouragement and reminding me that the path to success was not always linear. She shared stories of resilience and determination, instilling in me the belief that I had the power to achieve anything I set my mind to.

As the acceptance letters rolled in, I carefully weighed my options, considering the universities that aligned with my goals and offered the best opportunities for growth. Eventually, I made my decision and accepted an offer from the prestigious University of Southern Africa.

The anticipation of starting university filled me with a mix of nervousness and excitement. The thought of stepping into a new academic environment, meeting new people, and delving into a curriculum focused on entrepreneurship fueled my eagerness to embark on this new chapter.

With MaMokoena by my side, I packed my belongings and bid farewell to the familiar walls that had sheltered me during my gap year. As we walked out of the door, I couldn't help but feel a pang of nostalgia for the time spent in that cozy home. But I knew that this was just the beginning of my journey, and there were new horizons waiting to be explored.

Arriving at the university campus, I was greeted by a vibrant and bustling atmosphere. The energy and enthusiasm of fellow students filled the air, and I knew I had entered a world of endless possibilities. As I settled into my dormitory and attended orientation events, I was eager to immerse myself in the university experience and seize every opportunity that came my way.

Throughout my first year at university, I threw myself into my studies and extracurricular activities. I joined entrepreneurship clubs, attended networking events, and sought mentors who could guide me on my entrepreneurial journey. The university provided me with a wealth of resources and a supportive community of like-minded individuals who shared my passion for business.

As the months turned into years, I continued to grow and evolve, gaining valuable knowledge and skills that would shape my future. The university experience challenged me, pushing me to expand my horizons, think critically, and develop a deep understanding of the business world.

Looking back on my decision to take a gap year, I realized that it had been a transformative period of self-discovery. It had allowed me to reassess my passions, explore different paths, and ultimately find my true calling. Through the guidance and unwavering support of MaMokoena, I had discovered the courage to follow my dreams and pursue a future that resonated with my innermost desires.

As I prepared to enter my final year of university, I couldn't help but feel a profound sense of gratitude for the experiences that had brought me to this point. I knew that the journey was far from over, and there would be more challenges and triumphs awaiting me in the world of entrepreneurship.

But as I reflected on my time at St Louis Children's Home, the gap year, and my transition to university life, I recognized the valuable life lessons that had shaped me into the person I had become. The importance of resilience, self-discovery, and the support of loved ones were etched deeply into my being.

As I closed the chapter on my gap year and prepared to embrace the next phase of my journey, I carried with me the knowledge that true success comes from pursuing one's passions, following one's heart, and never losing sight of the transformative power of self-discovery. With these lessons in my arsenal, I was ready to embrace the challenges and opportunities that lay ahead, confident in my ability to carve my own path and create a meaningful legacy in the world of entrepreneurship.

Throughout my university years, Lebohang remained a steadfast friend and confidante. We supported each other through the ups and downs of academic life, celebrating each other's achievements and offering a shoulder to lean on during moments of doubt. Lebohang's unwavering belief in me and her constant encouragement were a source of strength that fueled my determination to succeed.

Together, we embarked on new ventures, collaborating on business ideas and challenging each other to think outside the box. We attended conferences and workshops, soaking up knowledge and inspiration from industry leaders and innovators. Through it all, our friendship continued to thrive, providing a solid foundation of trust, understanding, and shared aspirations.

As graduation approached, I couldn't help but feel a mix of excitement and nostalgia. The years had flown by, filled with countless lectures, late-night study sessions, and unforgettable moments of camaraderie. It was a time of immense growth and transformation, and I was ready to take the skills and knowledge I had acquired and apply them to real-world endeavors.

Lebohang and I had already started brainstorming business ideas, fueling our passion for entrepreneurship. We envisioned a future where we could make a meaningful impact on society, create innovative solutions, and empower others to chase their dreams. The world was our canvas, and we were determined to leave our mark.

As we walked across the stage, receiving our diplomas and stepping into the world as graduates, we knew that our journey was far from over. Armed with a solid education, a strong friendship, and an unwavering belief in ourselves, we were ready to face the challenges and uncertainties that awaited us.

Leaving the confines of the university campus, we set out to establish our own ventures. We worked tirelessly, pouring our hearts and souls into our respective businesses, leveraging our unique skills and experiences to build something remarkable. The road was not always smooth, and we encountered setbacks and obstacles along the way. But with every challenge, we grew stronger, learning valuable lessons that fueled our resilience and determination.

As the years went by, our businesses flourished, gaining recognition and making a tangible impact in our respective industries. Lebohang and I remained close allies, celebrating each other's successes and providing a support system during times of difficulty. Our bond had transcended friendship, evolving into a partnership built on trust, mutual respect, and a shared vision for the future.

Looking back on our journey from St Louis Children's Home to university and beyond, I couldn't help but marvel at the twists and turns that had led us to this point. The challenges, the losses, and the moments of triumph had shaped us into resilient individuals, capable of overcoming any obstacle.

In the face of adversity, we had learned the importance of perseverance and self-belief. We had discovered the power of forging meaningful connections and surrounding ourselves with individuals who lifted us higher. And through it all, we had never lost sight of the dreams and aspirations that had ignited our passion from the very beginning.

As the next chapter of our lives beckoned, we stood on the precipice of new possibilities, eager to continue our journey of entrepreneurship, innovation, and personal growth. The memories of our shared experiences and the lessons learned along the way would forever serve as guiding lights, reminding us of the strength and resilience we possessed.

And so, with hearts brimming with optimism and determination, Lebohang and I embarked on the next phase of our entrepreneurial odyssey. United by a shared vision and unwavering passion, we were ready to leave an indelible mark on the world, armed with the lessons of our past and the dreams of our future.

The adventure was far from over, and we were ready to embrace the unknown, confident in our ability to create a legacy that would inspire others and leave a lasting impact. Together, we ventured into uncharted territory, fueled by our shared determination to make a difference and create something extraordinary.

We immersed ourselves in the vibrant entrepreneurial ecosystem, attending conferences, networking events, and seeking mentorship from seasoned professionals. We absorbed knowledge like sponges, eagerly absorbing insights and strategies that would propel our ventures to new heights. The more we learned, the more our confidence grew, and the more we realized that our dreams were within reach.

Lebohang and I became a force to be reckoned with, combining our complementary skills and unique perspectives to tackle challenges head-on. We collaborated on projects, bouncing ideas off each other and providing constructive feedback. We became each other's sounding boards, always there to offer support, guidance, and a dose of motivation when the going got tough.

As our businesses flourished, we never forgot the values instilled in us during our time at St Louis Children's Home. We actively sought opportunities to give back to the community that had shaped us, supporting initiatives that uplifted underprivileged children and provided them with the resources and opportunities they deserved. We knew firsthand the transformative power of compassion and mentorship, and we were determined to pay it forward.

Throughout our journey, the memory of Noni lingered in our hearts. We carried her spirit with us, honoring her memory by embracing life to the fullest and seizing every opportunity that came our way. Her absence served as a constant reminder to cherish the moments we had and to be grateful for the connections we forged along the way.

Lebohang and I continued to push the boundaries of our ambitions, never settling for mediocrity. We were driven by a shared desire to make a meaningful impact and leave a legacy that extended far beyond ourselves. Our entrepreneurial endeavors became more than just businesses; they became platforms for change, catalysts for innovation, and sources of inspiration for aspiring entrepreneurs.

As the years went by, Lebohang and I achieved remarkable success in our respective ventures. Our businesses became household names, synonymous with innovation, excellence, and social responsibility. But more importantly, we had touched the lives of countless individuals, empowering them to pursue their own dreams and embrace their unique potential.

Looking back on our journey, from the halls of St Louis Children's Home to the heights of entrepreneurial success, I couldn't help but feel a profound sense of gratitude. Gratitude for the people who had believed in us, supported us, and lifted us up when we needed it most. Gratitude for the hardships we had faced, as they had molded us into resilient individuals capable of overcoming any obstacle. And most of all, gratitude for the friendship and bond that Lebohang and I shared, as it had been the bedrock of our journey.

As we stood on the precipice of new horizons, we knew that our story was far from over. The entrepreneurial path was ever-evolving, and we were eager to embrace the challenges and opportunities that lay ahead. With hearts aflame with passion and a shared commitment to making a difference, Lebohang and I were ready to step into the next chapter of our lives, confident that our friendship, resilience, and unwavering belief in ourselves would propel us to even greater heights.

And so, armed with the lessons of our past, the dreams of our future, and the enduring bond we shared, we embarked on this new chapter, ready to leave an indelible mark on the world and inspire others to chase their own dreams. The road ahead may be winding and unpredictable, but we knew that with each step, we were creating a legacy that would stand the test of time. And together, we were unstoppable.

Chapter 16

As Lebohang and I ventured further into our entrepreneurial journey, a beautiful love story began to unfold. Our deep connection and shared dreams had gradually blossomed into something more profound and magical. It was as if the universe had conspired to bring us together, intertwining our paths in a tapestry of love and destiny.

Our friendship, built on trust, support, and understanding, provided a solid foundation for our romantic feelings to flourish. We spent countless hours together, exploring the depths of our souls through conversations that were both profound and light-hearted. We laughed together, shared our dreams and fears, and discovered a profound sense of comfort and solace in each other's presence.

It was in the moments of quiet intimacy that we realized the depth of our feelings. The stolen glances, the gentle touch of hands, and the unspoken words that hung in the air—all served as testaments to the growing affection between us. We found ourselves drawn to each other's energy, as if our hearts recognized a kindred spirit in the other.

In the midst of our shared passions and aspirations, love had quietly taken root, blossoming like a delicate flower in the garden of our hearts. It was a love that transcended the ordinary, infused with the magic of companionship and a profound understanding of each other's dreams and ambitions.

As we navigated the complexities of our budding romance, we approached it with the same determination and resilience that had fueled our entrepreneurial endeavors. We understood that love, like any worthwhile endeavor, required patience, commitment, and a willingness to weather the storms that life inevitably brought our way.

Our love story unfolded against the backdrop of our shared adventures, whether it was conquering business challenges or championing causes close to our hearts. We celebrated each other's triumphs and provided unwavering support during moments of doubt or setbacks. Together, we faced the world as a united front, ready to overcome any obstacle that dared to challenge our love.

The beauty of our relationship lay not only in the joy and happiness we brought to each other's lives but also in the way our love expanded our horizons and encouraged personal growth. Lebohang inspired me to embrace vulnerability, to take risks, and to see the world through a lens of compassion and empathy. In turn, I encouraged her to believe in her own strength, to pursue her passions fearlessly, and to never settle for anything less than her dreams.

Our love story was a tapestry woven with moments of tenderness, passion, and unwavering support. We treasured the simple joys of holding hands, stealing kisses under the moonlit sky, and building a future filled with shared dreams and aspirations. With Lebohang by my side, life felt richer, brighter, and more meaningful.

As we embarked on this new chapter of our lives, love became the fuel that propelled us forward, igniting our creativity, and providing a sanctuary of love and warmth in a world that sometimes felt chaotic and uncertain. Our love was not only a source of personal happiness but also a force that inspired us to make a positive impact on the world around us.

Together, we dreamed of a future where our love would transcend boundaries, where our shared passions would create ripples of change, and where we would continue to support and uplift each other on our individual paths. Our love story was not just about us—it was about the transformative power of love itself, a force capable of creating beauty, inspiring growth, and reminding us of the incredible capacity of the human heart.

And so, as our love story unfolded, we embraced its magic and allowed it to guide us on a remarkable journey of self-discovery, personal growth, and boundless love. With each passing day, our love grew stronger, deeper, and more resilient, anchoring us in a bond that transcended time and space. We faced life's challenges together, drawing strength from our unwavering commitment to each other.

In the depths of our love, we found solace and a refuge from the chaos of the outside world. Lebohang became my rock, my confidante, and my biggest supporter. She believed in me when I doubted myself and pushed me to reach for the stars. In her presence, I felt seen, understood, and valued for who I truly was.

We embarked on countless adventures, creating memories that would forever be etched in our hearts. From spontaneous road trips to quiet evenings under the starlit sky, each moment was a testament to the depth of our connection. We laughed, we cried, and we celebrated life's victories, cherishing every precious second spent in each other's company.

But amidst the joy and bliss, we also faced our fair share of challenges. Life tested our resilience and commitment, presenting us with obstacles that threatened to shake the foundation of our love. Yet, through it all, we remained steadfast in our devotion, navigating the storms hand in hand.

Our love story was not without its lessons and growth. We learned the importance of communication, of listening with open hearts and understanding each other's needs and desires. We embraced vulnerability, allowing ourselves to be truly seen and known by the other. In doing so, our love deepened, blossoming into a profound and unbreakable bond.

As time passed, our love story continued to evolve. We pursued our individual dreams, supporting each other's ambitions and cheering each other on from the sidelines. We understood that true love was not about possession or stifling the other's growth, but rather about encouraging each other to reach for the stars and become the best versions of ourselves.

Lebohang became the muse behind my creativity, inspiring me to express my emotions through writing and art. Her unwavering belief in my talent pushed me to share my work with the world, and together, we celebrated every milestone and triumph along the way.

Our love story was a testament to the power of two souls intertwining in a dance of love, trust, and growth. It was a journey of discovering ourselves and each other, of embracing the beauty of imperfection and learning to forgive and heal. Together, we faced the complexities of life, armed with the unwavering strength of our love.

And so, as our love story continued to unfold, we knew that it was a rare and precious gift. We cherished each other, treasuring the depth of our connection and the immense joy we found in being together. In Lebohang's arms, I found my sanctuary—a place where I felt safe, loved, and understood.

Our love story was a tapestry woven with threads of laughter, tears, dreams, and passion. It was a love that defied boundaries, transcended expectations, and embraced the beauty of the imperfect human experience. With Lebohang by my side, I knew that I had found my soulmate, my partner in crime, and my forever love.

And as we stood hand in hand, ready to face the adventures that lay ahead, I knew that our love story would continue to unfold, weaving its magic into every chapter of our lives. Together, we would create a legacy of love, a story that would inspire others to believe in the transformative power of true connection.

For in our love, we had discovered a universe of endless possibilities—a love that would stand the test of time and illuminate our path, forever and always.

Chapter 17

As life unfolded before me, showering blessings upon my journey, there came a moment when I felt the overwhelming desire to give back, to express my deep gratitude to the person who had stood by my side through thick and thin. MaMokoena, the woman who had become a mother figure in my life, deserved to be honored in a special way.

With my heart filled with love and appreciation, I embarked on a mission to find a home—a place where MaMokoena could finally call her own. It was a daunting task, but the thought of seeing her happy and secure in a place she could truly call home fueled my determination.

After months of searching, I stumbled upon a quaint and cozy house that seemed to radiate warmth and comfort. It had all the qualities I envisioned for MaMokoena's new home—a tranquil garden, a spacious kitchen for her culinary creations, and a peaceful neighborhood where she could find solace.

Excitement coursed through my veins as I finalized the purchase, knowing that soon I would be able to surprise MaMokoena with the news. I meticulously planned every detail, eager to witness the joy and gratitude that would undoubtedly grace her face.

On a beautiful sunny day, I invited MaMokoena to join me for a stroll through a nearby park. As we strolled along the winding paths, our conversation flowed effortlessly, reminiscing about the cherished moments we had shared together.

Finally, as we found a quiet bench beneath the shade of a majestic tree, I took a deep breath and began to share my intentions. I expressed my deep gratitude for her unwavering love and support, recounting the countless ways she had touched my life and the lives of so many others.

With a trembling voice, I revealed my gift—a new home, a sanctuary where she could create new memories and find comfort in her golden years. Her eyes widened with disbelief, a mix of emotions washing over her face. Tears welled up in her eyes as she wrapped her arms around me, overwhelmed by the magnitude of the gesture.

In that heartfelt moment, we sat together, basking in the beauty of our connection. We laughed, we cried, and we marveled at the unpredictable twists and turns that life had taken us on. It was a testament to the power of love and the resilience of the human spirit.

As the days turned into weeks and weeks turned into months, MaMokoena settled into her new home, infusing it with her warmth and love. The walls echoed with the aromas of her delicious meals and the sound of her infectious laughter. It became a place where memories were made, stories were shared, and love was woven into every corner.

But amidst the joy of this new chapter, my heart yearned for something more. It whispered of a love that had blossomed and grown, a love that had stood the test of time. It was time to take another step on this journey of love, to make a commitment that would bind us together in an eternal bond.

With nerves tingling and love flowing through my veins, I approached Lebohang, the woman who had captured my heart and soul. In a moment of vulnerability, I bared my emotions, expressing my deepest desires and hopes for our future. I spoke of forever, of building a life together based on love, trust, and unwavering support.

Lebohang listened intently, her eyes filled with love and understanding. In that sacred moment, she reciprocated my feelings, expressing her own commitment to our shared path. We spoke of dreams, of a future intertwined, and of a love that knew no boundaries.

And so, in the warmth of our embrace, we sealed our love with a promise—a promise to embark on this journey together, hand in hand, embracing the joys and challenges that lie ahead. We knew that our love was a rare and precious gem, one that deserved to be cherished and nurtured.

With the blessings of our families and the support of our loved ones, we began the beautiful dance of planning our future. We discussed our dreams, aspirations, and the steps we needed to take to turn them into reality. The road ahead might be filled with uncertainties, but with each other by our side, we knew we could conquer anything.

As the seasons changed, our love continued to bloom, deepening with each passing day. We celebrated the small victories, cherished the quiet moments, and navigated the hurdles that life threw our way. Together, we created a sanctuary of love, trust, and mutual respect—a haven where we could be our authentic selves and grow individually and as a couple.

Lebohang became my rock, my confidante, and my best friend. She embraced my flaws and celebrated my strengths. In her presence, I found solace and inspiration, and together, we encouraged each other to reach for the stars.

As the years went by, we pursued our individual passions and carved our paths in the world. Lebohang excelled in her chosen field, making a difference in the lives of those she encountered. And I, guided by my deep-rooted desire to inspire and educate, found my calling as a philanthropist, molding young minds and imparting knowledge with passion and dedication.

Our love story continues to unfold, each chapter bringing new adventures, growth, and shared experiences. We have learned to navigate the challenges that life throws our way, holding onto each other tightly during the storms and rejoicing in the sunshine that follows.

And so, as I pen these words, I reflect on the journey that has brought me to this point—a journey filled with pain, loss, resilience, and love. From the depths of despair, I have risen, finding strength in the love of those who have crossed my path. Through their love, I have discovered my own capacity for resilience, compassion, and forgiveness.

As the chapters of my life continue to unfold, I am grateful for the lessons learned, the bonds formed, and the love that has carried me through. I embrace the unknown with open arms, knowing that the love I have found will guide me, inspire me, and bring me closer to the person I am meant to be.

For love is not simply an emotion or a fleeting feeling—it is a transformative force that has the power to heal, to inspire, and to shape our destinies. And as I embark on the next chapter of my life, I hold onto the belief that love will always be my guiding light, illuminating the path ahead with hope, joy, and endless possibilities.

Bonus Chapter: A Celebration of Love, Remembrance, and New Beginnings

The sun cast a golden glow over the beautifully decorated backyard, where laughter and the tantalizing scent of braaied meat filled the air. It was a momentous occasion—the long-awaited housewarming gathering at Lebohang and Mohlolo's new home. The event brought together the lives touched by their remarkable journey, along with the cherished memories of their childhood friends who were no longer physically present.

Thatelo, now a resilient young woman, stood at the heart of the celebration, surrounded by loved ones. She carried within her the memories of her late childhood friend, Prudence, who had departed too soon. Prudence's spirit lived on in the hearts of those who had known her, a guiding presence that reminded them of the preciousness of life and the enduring power of friendship.

Pontsho, Mohlolo's childhood companion, stood by his side, a pillar of unwavering support. Together, they reminisced about the adventures they had embarked upon, the dreams they had shared, and the challenges they had overcome. Their bond had stood the test of time, a testament to the lasting power of true friendship.

As the guests mingled and shared stories, their laughter echoed through the air. They celebrated not only the joy of a new home but also the resilience and love that had brought them to this point. They toasted to the unbreakable bonds forged through shared experiences, the laughter that had brought light to their darkest moments, and the strength they had discovered in one another.

Lebohang and Mohlolo, hand in hand, stood at the center of the gathering, their hearts brimming with gratitude. They looked back on the journey that had led them to this moment—a journey marked by both triumphs and heartaches. Their love had blossomed amidst the challenges they had faced, growing stronger with each hurdle they overcame.

In a heartfelt speech, Mohlolo expressed his gratitude for the presence of their loved ones and the unwavering support they had received. He acknowledged the memories of their departed friends, Prudence and Noni, whose spirits remained eternally intertwined with their lives. He spoke of the profound impact their friendships had made, the lessons they had learned, and the love that continued to shape their journey.

As the sun began to set, casting a warm glow over the gathering, they moved to the braai area, where the flames danced to the rhythm of their laughter and conversation. It was a moment of togetherness, a celebration of life and the unbreakable bonds that had been forged over the years.

In the midst of the festivities, they took a moment to honor the memory of their departed friends. They lit candles, their gentle flicker serving as a poignant reminder of the love and connection that transcended physical boundaries. In that sacred moment of remembrance, they found solace and strength, knowing that the memories of their friends would forever guide their paths.

As the evening continued, they shared stories of their childhood adventures, the dreams they had pursued, and the profound impact each person had made in their lives. They celebrated not only the memories of their departed friends but also the promise of new beginnings and the love that surrounded them.

With hearts filled with gratitude and hope, they raised their glasses in a collective toast. They celebrated the power of friendship, the resilience of the human spirit, and the transformative nature of love. They knew that their journey would continue, with each step forward marked by the love, support, and cherished memories of those who had touched their lives.

As the night gently embraced them, they bid their guests farewell, their hearts overflowing with gratitude. They retired to their new home, filled with a sense of profound contentment and anticipation for what lay ahead. As Lebohang and Mohlolo settled into their new home, they knew that this gathering marked not only a celebration but also a new chapter in their lives—a chapter that would be defined by love, growth, and shared dreams.

In the days that followed, Lebohang and Mohlolo reveled in the joy of their new space. They embraced the opportunity to create a home filled with warmth and love, a sanctuary where they could build a future together. They adorned the walls with photographs and mementos, each one a testament to the journeys they had taken and the people who had shaped their lives.

Thatelo, Pontsho, and the others continued to support and uplift one another as they navigated the challenges and triumphs of life. They shared laughter, tears, and dreams, forming an unbreakable bond that carried them through each day. Their friendship remained a beacon of light, a constant reminder of the strength found in connection and the power of love to heal.

As the years passed, their lives unfolded in beautiful and unexpected ways. Thatelo pursued her passion for education, becoming a dedicated teacher who touched the lives of countless young minds. Pontsho's artistic talents flourished, and he found success as a renowned painter, his canvases capturing the vibrant spirit of their shared experiences. They each carved their unique paths, but their connection remained unwavering.

Lebohang and Mohlolo's love continued to grow, evolving into a partnership rooted in trust, respect, and unwavering support. Together, they weathered the storms and celebrated the victories, their love serving as a guiding light in their journey. They found solace and strength in each other, knowing that their bond was unbreakable.

And on occasion, they would gather once again in that backyard—the place where their stories converged—and celebrate the milestones and joys that life bestowed upon them. They would light the braai fire, their laughter mingling with the crackling of the flames, as they embraced the gift of togetherness.

In those moments, they would remember their departed friends and loved ones, their spirits forever alive in their hearts. They would share stories and memories, ensuring that their legacies lived on. And amidst the celebration, they would honor the profound impact each person had made on their lives, knowing that they were forever connected by the ties of love and friendship.

For it was in these moments of celebration, amidst the laughter and the shared meals, that they found solace in the beauty of life's tapestry. They cherished the memories of the past, treasured the present, and looked forward to the future with hope and anticipation. Their journey, marked by love, resilience, and the enduring power of friendship, continued to unfold—one chapter at a time.

And as they stood together, hands clasped, hearts intertwined, they knew that their story was far from over. There were still adventures to be had, dreams to chase, and new chapters waiting to be written. With their spirits united and their love as their compass, they stepped forward into the unknown, ready to embrace whatever came their way.

For in the end, it was the love they shared, the memories they cherished, and the bonds they forged that would forever illuminate their path—a path guided by the beauty of their intertwined lives and the enduring power of love.

And so, they celebrated not only this moment but the infinite possibilities that lay ahead—the promise of a future filled with love, laughter, and the profound connections that would continue to shape their lives.

About the Author

Lebohang Phoshudi, born and bred in Theunissen on 02 March, is an aspiring author with a passion for storytelling. Growing up in a small town, Lebohang developed a deep appreciation for literature and the power of words to transport readers to different worlds.

From a young age, Lebohang was captivated by books and spent countless hours immersed in various genres, ranging from fantasy and science fiction to historical fiction and contemporary literature. This early love for reading sparked a desire to create original stories and share them with others.

Lebohang's writing journey began in high school when they started penning short stories and poems. These early attempts at storytelling allowed them to explore different writing styles and experiment with narrative techniques.

Lebohang also participated in writing workshops and joined local writing groups, connecting with fellow aspiring authors and learning from experienced writers. These interactions allowed them to receive valuable feedback, hone their writing abilities, and gain confidence in their unique voice.

Lebohang's writing style is characterized by vivid descriptions, compelling characters, and thought-provoking themes. They strive to create stories that resonate with readers, exploring universal emotions and experiences while also challenging societal norms and perceptions.

As an aspiring author, Lebohang dreams of publishing their own novel someday, hoping to transport readers to new worlds and provoke thought through their writing. They draw inspiration from a wide range of sources, including nature, personal experiences, and the diverse cultures and traditions they encountered growing up in Theunissen.

In addition to their passion for fiction, Lebohang is also keen on exploring non-fiction writing, particularly in the areas of social issues, personal development, and cultural exploration. They believe that writing has the power to educate, inspire, and foster empathy, and they aspire to contribute to these endeavors.

Lebohang Phoshudi's journey as an aspiring author is driven by a profound love for storytelling and a commitment to crafting narratives that entertain, enlighten, and provoke thought. With their talent, dedication, and determination, they are poised to make their mark on the literary world and captivate readers with their unique stories.

www.ingramcontent.com/pod-product-compliance
Lightning Source LLC
Chambersburg PA
CBHW061622130726
47996CB00003B/1089